Cincinnati Scenes

by *Caroline Williams*

CINCINNATI SCENES
CINCINNATI—STEEPLES, STREETS AND STEPS
THE CITY ON SEVEN HILLS
MIRRORED LANDMARKS OF CINCINNATI
AS ALWAYS, CINCINNATI

Cincinnati Scenes

Caroline Williams

LANDFALL PRESS, INC.
4077 E. Town & Country Rd.
Dayton, Ohio 45429

*"Cincinnati Scenes" is an expanded and revised edition of
"Cincinnati—Steeples, Streets and Steps," by Caroline Williams,
Copyright © 1962, 1968 by Caroline Williams*

*Most of the sketches in this book were
originally published in the Cincinnati Enquirer
under the title "A Spot in Cincinnati"*

*Published as a Landfall Press book
by arrangement with Doubleday & Co. Inc.,
who have authorized this edition.
October, 1973*

*Library of Congress Catalog Card Number 68–22507
Copyright © 1962, 1968 by Caroline Williams
All Rights Reserved
Printed in the United States of America
by
The C. J. Krehbiel Company
Cincinnati, Ohio*

ISBN NUMBER 0-913428-12-4

Grateful acknowledgment is given to

JANE FINNERAN

ELEANOR ADAMS

DOROTHY CALDWELL

*for their advice and assistance
in preparing this book.*

Foreword

T̲ʜᴇ ᴛʀᴜʟʏ ᴇxǫᴜɪsɪᴛᴇ sᴋᴇᴛᴄʜᴇs of Caroline Williams have graced the Sunday editorial pages of the Cincinnati *Enquirer* for many years.

They have chronicled in clean and fluent lines—in a manner seldom equaled anywhere—the history and charm of this region, its homes, its scenery and its many places of picturesque interest.

In this book, Miss Williams has singled out for drawing and brief description—many Cincinnati scenes. They combine some vistas still in existence, and others never again to be seen except through the artistry of her pen. Comparisons coupled with the flight of the years also are included.

I consider it a privilege to speak a foreword introducing this new assembly of Miss Williams' genius and craftsmanship. As always, she has captured with her pen not only the outline and detail but also the spirit and tradition of the buildings and places that make this heartland of America so dear to us all.

Her sketches, though, speak best for themselves.

Rᴏɢᴇʀ H. Fᴇʀɢᴇʀ
Former President and Publisher
The Cincinnati Enquirer, Inc.

Preface

This book of sketches made in and around Cincinnati is a rather random selection chosen from the many which have appeared over a period of years in the Cincinnati *Enquirer*. Most of the subjects are as sketched at the moment and will remain for quite a while. Some will be gone before too long. A few, which have already been swept from the scene as the newer day takes over, have been included as a bit of nostalgic memory.

It is hoped that the book will reflect something of the flavor of the city which, in a country that has almost a frightening monotony in some of its big cities, has always stood out as individual—with a background to give stability and a future to contemplate with hope.

It takes time to build a city—with plenty of work, infinite patience and, of course, many mistakes along the way. Each year, each generation leaves a bit of itself as a memento of the period. The ideas, ideals, the desires and plans and dreams of a people are hidden in the concrete, stone and wood that make up the city streets. The buildings are sometimes gay, often pathetic or sad examples of one generation's best efforts, disdained by the next, dwarfed by larger and grander but not always better efforts.

Cincinnati has always been a city which progressed slowly; remnants of its past have always stood bold and proud next to the new, open to admiration or ridicule. She has been called at various times: "a city with its foot in the past," "little old," "serene" and "conservative," but now, with a great hustle and rush, major changes are being made. Bricks are falling all around. Whole streets have disappeared. Blocks of buildings have been bulldozed out.

This is the period of the greatest transition the city has ever known, and the new city, anticipated with great interest, will reflect the taste of the present generation. It will be judged by the generations to come who will inherit the finished product and speak with respect or contempt for our foresight, just as we, today, criticize the past.

The sketches in the book are of Cincinnati as it is—the past and present—but the book does not pretend to present the whole picture. It does not contain the fine core area buildings, the schools, office buildings and stores which are a necessary part of city life and in which the town can match or surpass any metropolis its size. It presents, rather, some of the bits and pieces found around the corner—the streets which do not run straight, the steps climbing the rocky hillsides and the steeples which have stood against the skyline for a long, long time.

Caroline Williams

Contents

Cincinnati from the Kentucky Hills	*18*
The Suspension Bridge	*20*
The Bridge from the Public Landing	*22*
Race Street	*24*
The Beecher Home	*26*
Saint Peter's and the Plum Street Temple	*28*
The Tyler Davidson Fountain	*30*
A Cincinnati Hillside	*32*
The Taft Museum	*34*
From the Side of the Taft	*36*
East Fourth Street	*38*
The Thoms Building	*40*
Dayton Street	*42*
Saint Peter's Evangelical Protestant Church	*44*
Sacred Heart Academy	*46*
Antique Street	*48*
Along the Waterfront	*50*
Saint Paul's Church	*52*
Rookwood Pottery	*54*
The Union Terminal	*56*
The Winton Place Station	*58*
The City from Hughes Street	*60*
The Literary Club	*62*
Mount Adams from Covington	*64*
The Spires of Saint George	*66*
Corporation Alley	*68*
Steps from Liberty Street	*70*
The Kemper Log Cabin	*72*
West Sixth Street	*74*

Christ Church	76
A Covered Bridge	78
The Top of Mount Adams	80
The City from Mount Adams	82
Findlay Market	84
Over the Rhine	86
Republic Street	88
Steps Above Lang Street	90
Washington Park	92
Pitt Street	94
The Public Library	96
The Top of Sycamore Hill	98
The Boy on the Fountain	100
The Canal at Metamora	102
Baymiller Street	104
Cathedral of Saint Peter in Chains	106
The Isaac M. Wise Temple	108
The Cincinnati Woman's Club	110
Upper Main Street	112
The Eden Park Bridge	114
The City from the Hills	116
Mount Adams from Fort Washington Way	118
Music Hall	120
The Hamilton County Memorial Building	122
A Monument in Fort Thomas	124
The Covington Cathedral Basilica	126
Fourth Street	128
The Clock on Fourth Street	130
The College-Conservatory	132
Sixth Street Market	134
Saint Rose Church	136
An Old Mill	138
Crofton Drive	140
The Avalon	142

Stairs on Fort Washington Way	*144*
The Monument to Fort Washington	*146*
Tomb of William Henry Harrison	*148*
From Log Cabin to High-rise	*150*
Ortiz Alley	*152*
The Cincinnati Academy of Medicine	*154*
Elsinore Entrance	*156*
The University of Cincinnati	*158*
Hamer and Back Streets	*160*
Benton Street	*162*
From the Covenant-First Presbyterian Church	*164*
Elgin Place	*166*
Along the River	*168*
Aurora from Hillforest	*170*
The Fort Hamilton Monument	*172*
The Steeple of Philippus Church	*174*

Cincinnati Scenes

Cincinnati from the Kentucky Hills

The view of Cincinnati from Devou Park in Covington has remained substantially the same for the last decade or so. There has been a great deal of construction, but the new buildings have been swallowed up in the general pattern of the city, the river and the hills.

In the next few years the changes will begin to show, especially when the new stadium is completed. It is already under construction down by the old public landing. The new expressway distributor, Fort Washington Way, is finished across the town and the Brent Spence Bridge, which carries Interstate 75 from Kentucky into the city, opened in 1963. It is the first new bridge in sixty-seven years. Now there are five vehicular bridges over the Ohio, linking the two states into greater unity.

The Suspension Bridge

From all along the riverfront and from in between the houses on the lower streets of Covington, the Suspension Bridge can be seen rising against the Cincinnati skyline. This, the first of the bridges across the Ohio, is still the most graceful. It is the one photographed most often as the representative landmark of the city.

The suspended span was finished just after the Civil War when the emergency pontoon bridges had pointed up the great necessity for a quicker way to cross the dividing water. With the opening of the bridge the traffic flowed easily between the states, the trade barriers were broken and Cincinnati became "the Gateway to the South."

The Bridge from the Public Landing

From the public landing the tower at the southern end of the Suspension Bridge is seen rising above the Kentucky side of the river.

The fine old bridge is undisputed king of the waterfront and in 1966 when it reached the age of one hundred its birthday was observed by a gala series of celebrations.

It is hard to imagine the time when the people of Cincinnati, Covington and the surrounding areas were dependent on ferryboats to cross the barrier of water that so stubbornly separated the communities. There was talk of a bridge from the earliest days but it remained only arguments, plans and hopes until 1856 when construction for John A. Roebling's design for a suspension span was finally started. It was mainly a Kentucky project. Work had barely gotten under way when it was halted by a financial depression and the Civil War.

While it stopped the construction, the Civil War, with the constant threat of raids on Cincinnati by John Hunt Morgan and Kirby Smith, as well as the delays in transportation of supplies, gave the impetus needed for completion. When hostilities ended Cincinnati joined in to see that the bridge was finished.

The span opened to foot traffic in December of 1866 and, on New Year's Day, when vehicular traffic was started, they say forty-seven thousand people crossed from city to city.

It was the longest suspension bridge in the world at that time, antedating the Brooklyn Bridge, also designed by Roebling, by sixteen years. With or without a record, it is still the most important, the finest, of all the Ohio River bridges.

Race Street

In the very early days, before the village could even be called a town, they used to race up and down Race Street. And so it became a legend that that is how the street received its name. It seems more likely, however, that the street was named before the racing started, for the history books mention that it was marked on the map of the town-to-be made out by Israel Ludlow not long after the first little boatload of settlers landed at Yeatman's Cove.

All accounts do agree that the soldiers of Fort Washington and the sporting gentlemen of the village laid their wagers and then sped their horses up Race from the river to what is now McMicken Avenue. The sport was so popular, in fact, that by 1822 there was a fine of fifty dollars for starting a race within the town limits—that meant anyplace below our Seventh Street.

Race Street has grown up since then. The sketch shows a bit of the upper end as it appears from Washington Park, with stores, houses and churches crowding each other along the sidewalk.

The Beecher Home

Harriet beecher stowe, whom Lincoln once called "the little woman who started this big war," is said to have gathered material for her famous book, *Uncle Tom's Cabin*, at her father's home in Walnut Hills. Now a museum, the rambling brick house still stands on a knoll at the corner of busy Gilbert and Foraker avenues. It was built as a farmhouse in 1832 and was the home of the Reverend Lyman Beecher and his family when he came to Cincinnati to teach theology at nearby Lane Seminary.

Harriet was twenty-one when they arrived and she became a teacher at the Western Female Seminary founded by her sister Catherine. Here, too, she met and married a professor, Calvin Stowe. It was not until after they had moved to the East that she wrote her famous book (as well as many others not so well known) but it is said that her early anti-slavery sentiments were fostered by the lively discussions carried on by the abolitionists who frequented the home of the famous Beecher family.

Saint Peter's and the Plum Street Temple

Two of cincinnati's oldest buildings face each other at Eighth and Plum to form one of the city's most stately corners. Saint Peter in Chains Cathedral, built in 1845, and the Plum Street Temple, which followed twenty years later, are examples of the very best which former generations presented to the new city.

The corner has a fresh, bright look these days with Saint Peter's completely rebuilt and enlarged and the temple renovated and beautiful in its light gray paint. The core area is spreading out, new buildings rising rapidly all around, but these two brilliant landmarks of the city's history seem secure for many years to come.

The Tyler Davidson Fountain

It has been ninety-six years since the Tyler Davidson Fountain was put up on the Fifth Street esplanade, the nucleus of Fountain Square—a little oasis in a busy city—a breathing space among the buildings. It is called the center of the city, and, if not centered geographically, it is at least the heart of the business district. A picture of the fountain is often used as a symbol of the city itself.

Now the site is changing, the fountain relocated on a new plaza which tops an underground garage. New buildings are rising to form strange backgrounds for its aging beauty.

The fountain itself sits passively by as the construction and noise go on. It was built in the midst of argument and destruction. Back in 1872, when Henry Probasco offered the Bavarian-made piece of statuary to the city in honor of his brother-in-law, the site was in dispute. The space on Fifth Street was in the city plans as a perpetual marketplace, and special police had to guard the wreckers who took down the frame market house which stall-holders stubbornly refused to relinquish.

So the fountain may well be unconcerned. Soon it will be all settled again. The water will spray forth on a summer day, festive affairs will be celebrated around its base, civic drives given their send-off, and strangers will snap pictures as the fountain rises sedately in its new surroundings.

A Cincinnati Hillside

In a zigzag course ending at the monastery, the streets climb the steep hillside to Mount Adams in typical Cincinnati fashion. Few cities can offer such an involved pattern of streets and hills—or so many high vantage points from which to appreciate the finished effect.

In the sketch, the Ida Street Viaduct cuts across the top. Underneath runs East Court Street, while Elsinore branches off farther down. At the base of the hill East Court appears again as it meets Gilbert Avenue.

Soon the Northeast Expressway will run across the bottom of the hill. Many of the buildings on East Court and Gilbert are being razed to make way for the project.

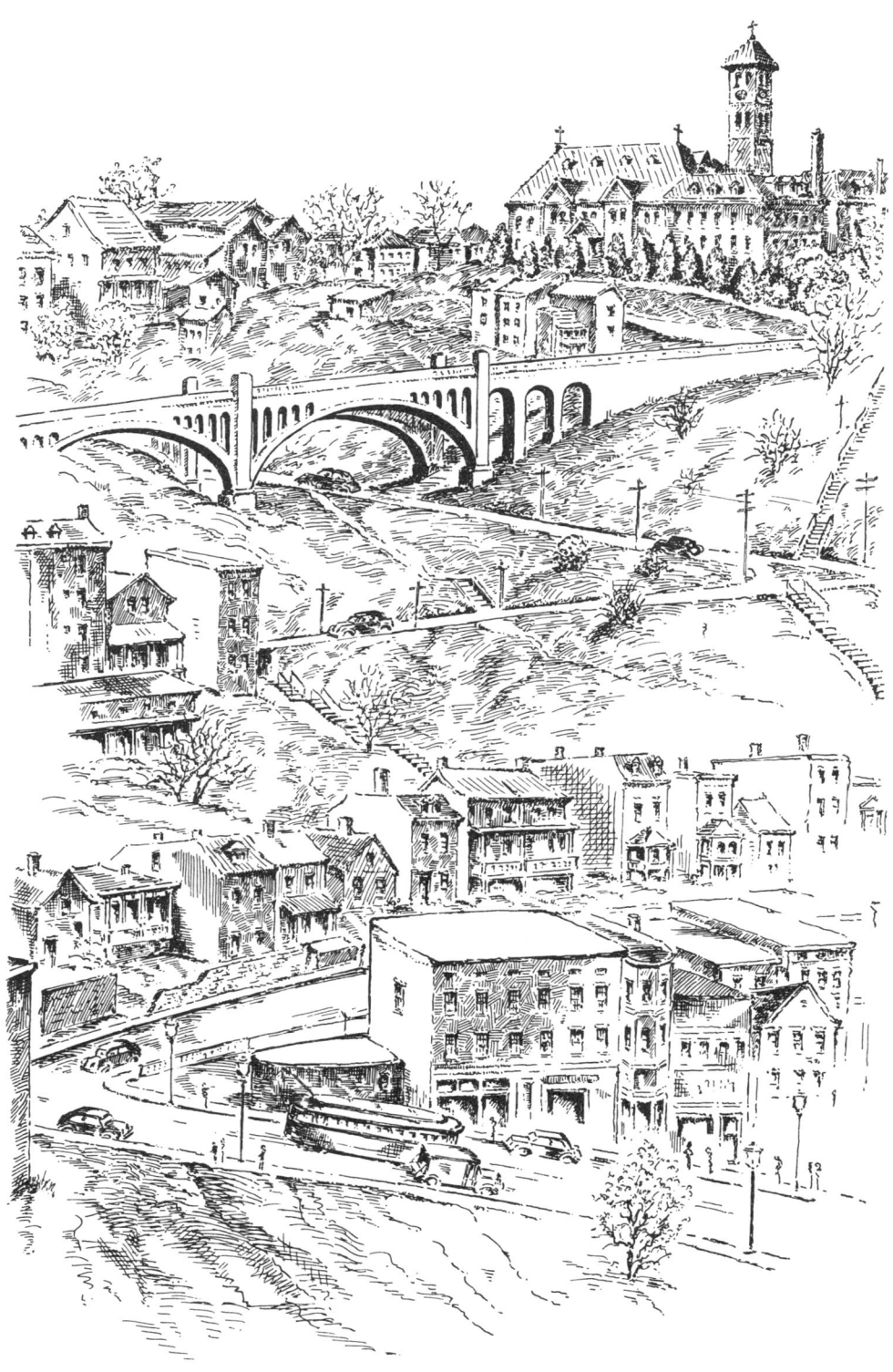

The Taft Museum

The beautiful Taft Museum—home of the Cincinnati Institute of Fine Arts—offers a glimpse into the city's bygone days. Restored to its earliest period, the house exemplifies a mode of gracious living achieved by a few of the pioneer citizens. It is one of the finest examples of Early Federal architecture in the nation. Here, at Fourth and Pike, beauty and history now combine to perpetuate a perfect setting for the art treasures on display.

The history of the place is well known. It was built about 1820 by Martin Baum and probably designed by the architect Benjamin Latrobe. Next it became "Belmont," a private school, until it was purchased by Nicholas Longworth, who later sold it to David Sinton. Finally it became the home of Charles Phelps Taft, the brother of William Howard Taft, who became the twenty-seventh President of the United States.

The Tafts, during their long tenure in the home, acquired a magnificent art collection, which, along with the house, they deeded to the city as a museum in 1927.

From the Side of the Taft

From the side entrance of the Taft Museum, Mount Adams can be seen rising above Columbia Parkway.

When the city was young, and the home new, the view was unobstructed, the hillside covered with trees and grapevines—all part of the extensive grounds which spread out and around the house.

Martin Baum had the first ornamental garden and the first vineyard in the town, when he owned the estate. Then Nicholas Longworth developed the grapevines up and over the hill which is now Mount Adams and Eden Park, helping with his experimental work to make Cincinnati for a time one of the largest wine-producing cities in the United States.

Now the house sits in a crowded city area, the one-time estate built up with houses, factories and highways.

East Fourth Street

For many, many years the beautiful gates of the Taft Museum framed a view of East Fourth Street and the gracious nineteenth-century homes which stood in a row facing Lytle Park. Touched with a charm which only time could bring, the group of houses formed a pleasant background for the park and an appropriate approach to the museum. It was the only residential block of its type left in Cincinnati, the houses finding their place in the present-day world as clubs, offices and apartments.

Now the new expressway is cutting underneath this area and the buildings are gone. Present plans promise that Lytle Park will be re-established after the construction work is finished. Cincinnatians who have a feeling for the past hope the houses too will be rebuilt to preserve a sample of an older day in the midst of a growing city.

The Thoms Building

The little old Thoms Building, which stood at Fifth and Main, is gone—the new Federal Building has taken over its corner. It is well worth a moment's remembering and a salute for the one hundred and thirty-three years it evaded the inroads of progress and remained stubbornly on the busy corner just off Government Square. Although the walls were exceptionally thick and the building sturdy, architecturally the place was of minor importance—in appearance, indistinguishable from the innumerable other squat red brick buildings scattered over the town.

Historically, it might be called Cincinnati's first skyscraper for in its day it was the tallest building around. In 1829, when there was plenty of room to spread out and height was unnecessary, head-wagging neighbors looked upon a structure of four stories with the gravest doubts. They glumly predicted that it would not stand long, but would collapse from its height.

When its day came, sidewalk superintendents watched the workmen struggling with the demolition with something like glee. They were obviously on the side of the building. Mr. Thoms had built well. His building became a major problem for the wrecking crew.

The sundial from the corner of the building was saved and today can be seen on the side of the gleaming new government building with a simple inscription. It is a surprisingly satisfactory memorial.

Dayton Street

Dayton street, most elegant of the residential streets of the old West End, is now specified by the city as a protection area. The lovely old homes will be preserved and no further commercial encroachment will be allowed, so that today's generation and the generations to come will have an example of mid-nineteenth-century town houses in their midst.

The places were built by wealthy families, well known in the financial history of the community; men involved in manufacturing, breweries and meat packing. The block between Baymiller and Lynn became known as "Millionaires' Row." Here there were formal gardens, yards enclosed by sturdy wrought-iron fences, carriage houses and porticoes. Dignity, not flashy display was the style, but elaborate detail is evident on most of the stone-fronted buildings.

Great interest has been taken in the neighborhood since the city announced that it would be preserved, the tree-shaded street inducing a nostalgic atmosphere of horse and buggy days, of gaslights, cobblestone streets, well-scrubbed stoops and leisure on a summer day.

Saint Peter's Evangelical Protestant Church

Saint peter's Evangelical Protestant Church, at the corner of McMicken and Main, has lost its rooster, its steeple, and its congregation. It is now simply a large, blunt, red brick building which juts out conspicuously at the intersection. It is used as a boys' club. Until quite recently the old church had its steeple and, atop the spire, a great golden rooster which was seen and known as an endearing landmark by all who passed through the northern end of town.

Here the quaint five-foot cock, symbol of Saint Peter, the patron saint of the congregation, is seen as it appeared on a winter day from Fourteenth Street. It topped a steeple built in 1870. Earlier still the church had boasted the city's tallest spire, blown off in a tornado in 1869.

Sacred Heart Academy

When William C. Neff built his home in Clifton in 1868 it is said he designed the place as a copy of the historic English castle Kenilworth. Elaborate care was taken with details from portico to interior trim. Swiss wood-carvers worked for two years cutting the intricate designs on the woodwork. That was the fashion of the day.

It was in the 1860s that some of the most pretentious suburban homes the city has ever known were built. Great fortunes were being accumulated, and men who had grown prosperous were leaving the downtown section to build fabulous mansions surrounded by acres of grounds farther out.

Now the extensive estates have been cut up, many of the old homes, which could not be duplicated at any price in today's market, demolished. But the Neff castle on Lafayette Avenue has been preserved as the central building of the Academy of the Sacred Heart. Many additions have been made since the girls' school moved here from Grandin Road in 1876, but the place still stands on its forty-seven acres of rolling land.

Antique Street

One of cincinnati's most picturesque byways bears the intriguing name of Antique Street. No one seems to know how or by whom it was named. But the name is appropriate. There is an atmosphere of great age, of quiet habitation, as the long shadows of old buildings fall across the narrow, rough roadway. A hillside street, just one block long, it climbs from East Clifton Avenue to the intersection of Peete Street and the base of the steps that rise above the end of Main Street. Peete Street cuts off to the left to wind around the edge of the hill.

Along the Waterfront

It is a crowded scene along the riverfront these days. The boats are packed in close together under the Central Bridge.

There is also a new addition to the public landing—the showboat *Majestic*. Cincinnati, long noted as a showboat town, now has one all her own. The city has purchased the *Majestic*, along with her own little tug, named the *Attaboy*. It's a boat with an interesting career—the longest history of any river showboat. Built in 1923 and for thirty-six years owned by the Reynolds family, it played old-time melodrama to packed houses up and down the rivers and streams of Kentucky, Ohio, West Virginia and Tennessee. Nine years ago it was sold to the Department of Theater at Indiana University. Now it belongs to Cincinnati and will have a permanent home on the waterfront.

Saint Paul's Church

THE OLD WEST END is now just a memory—the squalor and dirt of recent years, with the bright spots of its pretentious past shining through the soot, the melancholy grandeur of its prosperous days visible through the neglect.

Saint Paul's Methodist Episcopal Church was one of the stately relics of the district. Built in 1870, here it stood proud and resplendent and clean in the time of carriages and gaslights and cobblestone streets. It ranked with the best in the city, standing among the finest of the town houses with their ornate entrances and elaborate interiors, and noted for its fashionable parishioners and their glittering weddings. The old church, after several changes in congregations, gave way to progress in 1960, still sturdy and sound and holding its head high even as the wreckers battered away at its solid stone walls.

Rookwood Pottery

The pottery made by "Rookwood" was one of Cincinnati's world-famous products. Designed by some of the city's finest artists, executed by craftsmen with the most exacting care, the unique and beautiful glazed earthenware produced on the tip of Mount Adams took prizes all over the world. The enterprise was started in 1880 by Mrs. Maria Longworth Storer, daughter of Joseph Longworth, using Ohio Valley clay for ceramic products. In 1892 the present group of buildings was built next to the lamented old Mount Adams Incline and named Rookwood after the family estate.

Today the pottery is closed, the high standard of its products having made it impossible to compete with mass-production methods. The ever familiar buildings are used for offices.

The Union Terminal

In recent years Cincinnati's Union Terminal has become a problem child. What does one do with a railroad station when the public travels by car, air and bus? The place had always been called "the showplace of the Midwest," and "the city's most elegant structure." Then the words changed and the expressive phrase "a white elephant of noble proportions" caught on as a popular description. Too often the words "tear it down" were heard.

The terminal undoubtedly is and has been the most beautiful station in the nation. And the most efficient. The building was finished in 1933 at a cost of about nine million dollars in a complex that cost forty-one or -two million. No one cares to estimate what it would cost to duplicate it today. In the huge rotunda and along the concourse lights play upon fascinating inlaid Italian murals that depict the principal industries of Cincinnati as well as the history of transportation. There are shops, game rooms, a movie and restaurants, busy places for many years. The peak traffic was reached during the Second World War when almost two hundred trains a day arrived and departed and soldiers with their relatives and friends milled around the huge concourse or watched the elaborate fountain display out in front. Now the number of trains has dwindled to twenty-six and passengers seem lost in the vacant space.

Happily, after all the turmoil and discussion, the Center of Science and Industry has moved in and given the terminal new life. The newly formed center, dedicated to learning by discovery, has grown by leaps and bounds since it was formed just a few years ago. Thousands of people have flocked to its exhibits. Possibly it can take over the whole first floor in a few years.

The Winton Place Station

The beautiful Union Terminal may inspire admiration but it is a dreamy, affectionate nostalgia that surrounds the little old Winton Place Station. It seems, from its widespread popularity, that everyone in town must have met or boarded a train at Spring Grove Avenue at some time.

The small red and black station isn't much as buildings go—rough floors, worn benches in a small waiting room, the drab walls dotted with notices and signs, the old brick platform. The whole thing vibrates as the trains come through. But it holds memories, recollections of comings and goings, farewells and welcomes. It has been a very busy place, serving all the hilltop area since 1872.

Last year, after midnight on a hot August night, a group of devoted fans gathered at the depot to watch a train go through. It was supposed to be the last train before the place was closed for eighteen months so that the grade crossing could be eliminated. No doubt there would have been a much larger crowd if anyone had known that before the time was up the closing would be made permanent. Now the building is for sale, with the understanding that it will be moved and preserved in some other location.

The Baltimore and Ohio Railroad owns the depot, and shared it with the New York Central until the Union Terminal was built. Then it was made a stop for all passenger trains using that route.

The suburb, Winton Place, named for Matthew Winton, a pioneer tavern keeper on the riverfront, was just a little collection of homes when the railroad first came through. Chester Park, the amusement center across the street from the stop, was much better known, so it was called Chester Park Station for many years before it became officially the Winton Place Station.

The City from Hughes Street

Uptown and downtown—it all blends together from Hughes Street. Here the narrow residential street which runs from Mulberry to Liberty seems to end with the towers of the city right at its doorstep.

It is the name "Hughes" which is the reminder that when Cincinnati was young this was a long way from town and trees hid the view of the village. This was farmland, and here Thomas Hughes owned twenty-seven open acres. Hughes, along with his neighbor William Woodward, bequeathed money to the city for the education of poor children, and today Hughes and Woodward High Schools perpetuate the names of these early settlers while the growing metropolis has completely swallowed up their land.

The Literary Club

The Literary Club meets in a little brick house on East Fourth Street. It would be a lovely place if it stood all alone on a spacious lawn. With the massive Western and Southern on one side, the Phelps Apartments on the other, it has been made even more conspicuous and charming by being so much smaller than it neighbors.

The house was built around 1820 on the site of the home of Colonel Winthrop Sargent, Secretary of the Northwest Territory, and faces Lytle Park, the land where the soldiers of old Fort Washington drilled so long ago.

It is an appropriate home for the Literary Club, which is the oldest organization of its kind in the country, dating back to October of 1849 when twelve young men met and formed the society. Very few weekly meetings have been cancelled during its long existence except for an intermission of some three years during the Civil War. At that time, the week after Fort Sumter was fired upon, the club disbanded to form a military company known as the "Burnet Rifles." Fifty-one members went to war, under the command of Rutherford B. Hayes, a fellow member who later became President of the United States.

The roster of the club has always been limited to one hundred but, through the years, the membership has included many of the most distinguished names in the city's history.

Mount Adams from Covington

Mount Adams has always been, and remains, the most picturesque of the hilltops that surround the city. It is the easternmost of the semicircle of hills and the most individual. Its position, overlooking, and so close to, the downtown district, has made its history intertwined with that of the basin area; as the city grew so the craggy slopes changed from vineyards to suburban homesites. During the Civil War its promontory made it the natural site for fortifications to protect the surrounding territory from possible attack.

The view is the best from Covington, where the Ohio River, the bridges and the mouth of the Licking form a foreground for the church-topped hill as it rises high against the sky, clear cut or fading as the seasons change. It was from along here that Thomas and Samuel Kennedy carried passengers, horses and livestock back and forth across the river on the settlements' first ferryboat. In those pioneer days if the boatmen and their customers looked up they saw a hillside entirely covered by trees, with no buildings to break the outline, no bridges to span the water.

The Spires of Saint George

The graceful spires of Saint George Church as visible from many parts of the city. Here, sketched from a window in Christ Hospital, they tower over the snow-covered roofs of the hillside houses. Located on Calhoun Street near Vine, the church stands in the heart of Corryville, a small section named for the first mayor of Cincinnati, William Corry, whose home was nearby. When it was built in 1872, Saint George gathered its congregation from Mount Auburn, Clifton and Fairview Heights, for it was the first Catholic church on the hilltop.

Corporation Alley

When seventh street was known as Northern Row and marked the edge of the well-populated section of town, Liberty Street was the boundary of the corporate limits.

Until 1849 the "Liberty" in Liberty Street indicated to one and all that the laws of the town could not be enforced beyond that point. Anyone with a desire to break the Sunday ordinances, to drink or gamble, had only to cross the street to be out of the reach of whatever officers there were in the small town. For Cincinnati was just a small town then, and out here it was farmland, a house here and there, chickens and cows and, of course, hogs running loose up the hills and through the streets. The name of little Corporation Alley, which runs from Highland Avenue to Cumber Street along the hill, is just one more reminder of the town limits in those far-off days.

Steps from Liberty Street

From liberty street hill the land drops abruptly into a section of houses, shops and churches—the northern end of the basin area. A long flight of steps near the Pendleton house runs down the slope to the compact row of homes on Dandridge Street.

As a foreground for the downtown buildings, the rounded tower and the rooftop of Saint Paul Church at East Twelfth and Spring streets stand high above the surroundings. The familiar landmark and dominant structure in the neighborhood was built in 1850 when the streets were sparsely settled. But the parish grew and, at the turn of the century, a program to refurbish and redecorate the old church was started. In 1899, just as the work was finished, a fire raced through the building, leaving only the walls and foundation. Immediately it was reconstructed and dedicated again in 1900.

The Kemper Log Cabin

Standing as Cincinnati's oldest house, in fact the oldest within the Miami Purchase, and a valuable example of pioneer life, we have the well-known Kemper log cabin at the Zoo. It is not a replica but the original home built by the Reverend James Kemper about 1804. It was carefully moved from its site on Kemper Lane in 1913, the great squared logs taken down and then replaced in their original position one by one.

James Kemper came to Ohio in 1791 as pastor of the First Presbyterian Church in the struggling little river community. After a few years downtown, he moved his family over the hill to what is now Walnut Hills, the suburb taking its name from his one-hundred-and-fifty-acre farm. Here he remained, preaching and teaching and raising his fifteen children. For several years the family lived in a blockhouse, but when the danger of marauding Indians lessened, he built his log house close by. His children all grew to maturity and members of the family continued to occupy the home long after he was gone.

West Sixth Street

Wᴇsᴛ sɪxᴛʜ sᴛʀᴇᴇᴛ is now just another street—wider than most and cluttered up with parked cars. Yesterday it was a colorful, busy bartering place with its two sprawling market houses filling the center of the blocks from Elm Street to Central Avenue. Not a brick, stone or cabbage leaf remains to recall the old buildings which for all the years had seemed the most ineradicable part of the district.

Along the sidewalk, however, some of the old flavor of the area still exists. From the new parking garage one can see, across the street, the taller buildings rising above the old red brick stores and busy doorways where housewives can still feel and smell the vegetables displayed in awning-covered stalls.

Christ Church

Since 1835 Christ Church has spread around the corner of Fourth and Sycamore, watching the city grow, the pace quicken, as the area changed and the surrounding structures grew taller and bigger.

Following the trend, the old building, which has been home to the congregation all the many years, was torn down with nostalgic regret and a new, modern church was dedicated on April 14, 1957.

A Covered Bridge

Horses and buggies and a slow tempo, a quiet day on a country road, a rural Christmas card snow scene—of all the relics of the past which have survived the rush of progress, a covered bridge seems to trigger the most nostalgic memories.

Someone once wrote that bridges were covered to hide the ugliness of the nearby town from approaching travelers but, for the nostalgic, they will always be known as the kissin' bridges.

New England realized the sentimental importance of her bridges too late and is now hurrying to preserve the few which remain. Surprisingly enough, Ohio ranks high among the states in the number still standing and, while Hamilton County has only one, nearby Clermont County boasts of quite a few. The sketch shows one, in excellent condition, which crosses Stonelick Creek near Perintown, Ohio.

The Top of Mount Adams

It is all up and down in Mount Adams. Up from Jerome Street the steps of Saint Paul Place ascend toward the monastery. From the top, one looks across the ravine to the Church of the Immaculate Conception and down on the roofs and chimney tops of the houses clinging to the slope.

The church is probably known by more people than any other in Cincinnati and there is a feeling of real affection for the quaint little place built of stone quarried right from the rugged craig on which it stands.

Dedicated in 1860, its widespread fame comes from a Good Friday custom of "praying up the steps," a ceremony which has been observed every year of its existence. At one minute after midnight of Holy Thursday they start, penitents from all over the city, rain or shine, to climb the one hundred and eleven steps, to pause on the seven platforms, and finally reach the shrine at the top. As many as twenty-five thousand people have been known to make the pilgrimage on a Good Friday, people of many faiths joining their Catholic friends for an observance which has become a bit of religious history.

The City from Mount Adams

Some people only know Mount Adams from a distance, as a silhouette against the sky. Others are familiar with the suburb as the best vantage point from which to view the scene below.

In the sketch, the city is seen from the top of the steps which run from Saint Gregory Street to the Church of the Immaculate Conception—the steps which are climbed by thousands of persons each year in the annual Good Friday observance of the Pilgrimage of the Holy Cross.

With the great new influx of building on the hilltop, there is now fear that many of the panoramic views will be blocked. It is becoming increasingly necessary to restrict the height, width and position of new construction to protect the charm of the present properties.

Findlay Market

One by one the markets go. Now only Findlay remains—the last of the roof-covered establishments. Once they were scattered all around town but, as the city grew more crowded and traffic became a major problem, the space was usurped for wider streets and parking meters.

Findlay Market was started in 1852 when a market house of iron was erected on Elder Street. It was to be maintained forever in commemoration of the pioneer groceryman James Findlay. The place has been altered and rebuilt in its century of business, but today the great-grandsons of some of the original stall-holders often sell to the descendants of their early customers, and the cheerful price-haggling, the sing-song hawking of wares, the familiar smells and sounds and color that are the inevitable trappings of marketplaces continue to draw buyers from all over the city.

Over the Rhine

When the area north of the canal was "more German than Germany itself," they built their buildings fancy. A fine old relic of these flourishing days Over the Rhine stands at Twelfth and Walnut. Here, for the pleasure of those who care to look up, is a statue of Columbia, larger than life, in a niche over the doorway of the building, with every bit of the surface of the surrounding façade covered with scrolls and carvings. Interestingly enough, they say she was not Columbia originally but, when new, in 1878, represented Germania with a sword in her hand. When the First World War came along and the German youth of the neighborhood trooped off to war with all the rest of Cincinnati and German books were taken out of the library, the language dropped from the schools, the statue was draped in canvas and hidden from the public view. After the conflict she appeared again remodeled into Columbia. She is a favorite around here. The insurance company that owned her tells of the irate phone calls they received when some irreverent workmen, painting the building, put a lighted cigarette in her mouth, and the complaints when too many pigeons roost in her niche.

Nearby, on Vine Street, another remnant of the times is the fading building which housed Wielert's beer garden. It was a favorite among the many along Vine but is chiefly remembered because it was here that Boss George B. Cox ate his noonday lunch. At a table always reserved for him, surrounded by his lieutenants, many a vital decision was made in the civic affairs of the city.

Republic Street

Cincinnati, north of the canal, was not all beer gardens, theaters and song in the old days. That is the way it is remembered today—Over the Rhine in its heyday—when Cincinnati was known as the "wettest" city in the country. It was the night-life section, a place frequented by outsiders, with a conglomeration of memories of gaiety and gambling, wienerwurst and sauerkraut, plenty to drink and German concert bands. But it was just one bit of the picture, a small stretch concentrated more or less on Vine Street between the canal and Fifteenth Street.

The real backbone of the Over the Rhine community was the blocks and blocks of close-packed houses where the hard-working people lived among their shops and schools and many churches. It extended back to the base of the hills and climbed the slopes. And it was overcrowded. It was filled with solid brick houses, built flush with the sidewalks, walled gardens in the rear, tall shuttered windows, enclosed porches upstairs, recessed doorways. Here, in the morning, women scrubbed the front stoops on which the good German burghers sat in the evening, smoking long pipes, gossiping with neighbors, while youngsters carried pitchers of beer home from the corner saloons.

Republic Street ran through the community, all the way from Twelfth Street to Findlay. It was called Breman Street, or sometimes Strasse. From Elder Street near Findlay Market the street looks much as it did then, with Saint Johannes Church, built in 1845, still hovering over the houses.

Steps Above Lang Street

Quantities of cement and the engineering skill developed through years of experience have made short work of the problem involved in crossing Cincinnati's perpendicular hillsides. From Mulberry, at the end of Lang Street, a long flight of steps to Seitz Street can be seen staggering over the slope that is much too steep for vehicular traffic.

Lang Street has the distinction of being listed as the second-steepest street in the city. The only one with a steeper grade is Clyde Street, a little block-long stretch of hillside, with no houses, off River Road.

In the early days homeowners built wooden stairways to solve their problem, but soon the city and cement took over. Today, with some twenty-five miles of steps to keep in good repair, the highway maintenance department makes its own precast concrete replacements ready to use as fast as the flat surfaces are worn away by the countless walking weary feet of the hill climbers.

Washington Park

Little old Washington Park, which stands across from Music Hall, is so small that it is probably overlooked by the great majority of Cincinnatians. Its charm is realized more fully from the inside looking out, where Saint John's Unitarian Church, at the corner of Twelfth and Elm, is but one of the many beautiful buildings which can be seen framed in a network of trees.

Saint John's served the oldest German Protestant congregation in the city. In more recent years the gray brick building has changed hands several times. It is now the Bethlehem Temple Church.

The park is older than the church or Music Hall or most of the buildings which surround and dwarf it. It was acquired in 1855, a few acres in the Over the Rhine section, set aside for a bit of rest, play and a walk, in a day when a Sunday afternoon stroll around the neighborhood was relaxation enough for the leisure time.

Pitt Street

Pitt street runs up a hillside in the Corryville area. It's a pretty little alleyway with a cobblestone surface, a steep ascent at the end and the old gaslighted lampposts which are becoming rather rare these days. The picturesque street starts at Vine across from Inwood Park and angles up to McMillan, a shortcut between the two main thoroughfares, which meet a few blocks farther up.

The street offers one more bit of variety to the bordering neighborhoods that enhance the changing aspect of Vine Street as it travels its nine miles from the river, past the skyscrapers and the closely packed downtown section, out through suburban areas and the industrial districts to end at Wyoming and the city's edge.

The Public Library

Bright, airy and spacious, the new public library at Eighth and Vine opened its doors in 1955. Here, in an innovation in library design, there are terraces, glass walls, a small formal garden with a serpentine brick wall and a magnolia tree which blooms in the spring. Soft music fills the air during the noon hour.

This, the main branch of the Cincinnati and Hamilton County system, is the latest step in a long progression which started back in 1802 when a few men met in Yeatman's Tavern to make plans for lending books to the public.

Many Cincinnatians were sentimentally attached to the old place on Vine, dingy as it was in its last days. For eighty-five years it stood next to the *Enquirer*. It was familiar and therefore dear—from the heads of Franklin, Shakespeare and Milton in stone replica at the entrance, to the marble floors and broad steps in the central hall surrounded by tier on tier of dark old stacks reached by narrow, circular iron stairways. It has been replaced by a parking lot and is almost forgotten.

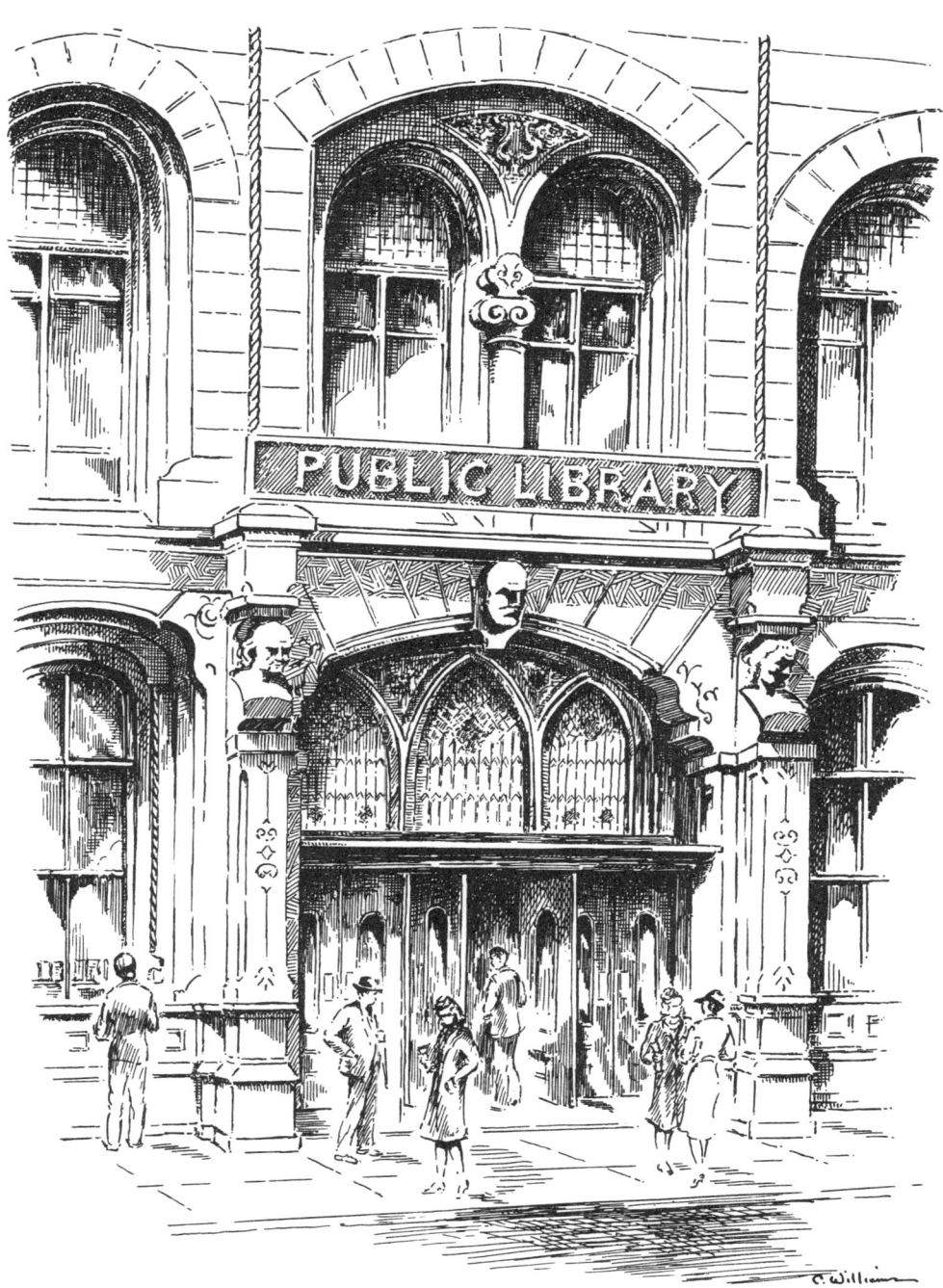

The Top of Sycamore Hill

Edinburgh Place never seems to change. A short and narrow cul-de-sac, one block long, it runs across the top of Sycamore Hill, the top floors of its buildings facing Dorchester Street, its rear windows and lower floors overlooking the city below.

Some of the balconies which once hung to the tall brick houses seem to have disappeared, but the steps, the stone walls and inevitable clotheslines are essentially just as they have been for many years. It is the view familiar to all the people who drive up the steep, straight hill to Mount Auburn.

The Boy on the Fountain

Each year at Christmastime the esplanade on Fountain Square is all decked out for the holidays. The trees and decorations may vary in size and trim, but the atmosphere is always gay. It is one of the happiest civic affairs perpetuated in the city.

The cold little boys on the fountain sit under the Christmas trees with never a shiver as the frosty wind blows. In December it's overcoat weather on the square but "the boy with the dolphin" and his scantily clothed companions (who, by the way, never admit they are ninety-six years old) accept the freezing spray with fixed smiles, seemingly pleased with the festive season.

The Canal at Metamora

THE OLD CANAL has been gone from the Cincinnati area for a long time, but the water still flows in one little section of the system in Indiana, passing right through the town of Metamora just off U. S. Highway 52. This is all that remains of the eighty-mile Whitewater Canal, which opened in 1843 from Cincinnati to Cambridge, Indiana, as the superhighway of its day. It was considered the all-time solution to the transportation problem. A fifteen-mile stretch of the waterway, as well as the unusual wooden aqueduct that carries the canal over Duck Creek, has now been restored as a state memorial to the old towpath days.

The Metamora Christian Church, standing so close to the water, is just about the same age as the canal. The congregation was formed in 1841, and the church built a little later on land given for the purpose by Henry Pond.

Baymiller Street

So BAYMILLER STREET dwindles to a path and stops. The old directories show that once, after a long straight course across town, it reached Central Avenue and ended at the canal. Then, when the canal was abandoned and Central Parkway built along its bed, they extended old Baymiller as a pedestrian concrete overpass high above the traffic. From there steps climb to McMicken, then Klotter, to Conroy, and end in the side of the hill topped by Fairview Heights.

The sudden transition from straight roadway to staggering flights of steps is an old habit with Cincinnati streets, an annoyance perhaps to the map-following motorist, but the typical gesture of defiance, the "never let a hill stop you" attitude of our streets and people.

Cathedral of Saint Peter in Chains

From Plum Street, the Cathedral of Saint Peter in Chains is seen next to the City Hall, the darker, sturdier structure of the civic building acting as a foil for the graceful spire of the church.

Saint Peter's was built in 1845. In 1938, following the general trend to the suburbs, Saint Monica in Clifton became the cathedral and the old church became Saint Peter in Chains. Then, in 1957 it was restored to its former high position. Revitalized, rebuilt, more beautiful than ever, it opened its doors again as cathedral for the Cincinnati archdiocese.

The City Hall in the background has been cleaned and all spruced up. Not as old as the cathedral, it is still a definite landmark in the city's growth. Opened in 1893 after six years of construction, the massive granite and sandstone building, with its turrets, towers and frescoes, is a grand old example of turn of the century architecture. The interior is admittedly insufficient for the needs of an ever growing government, but so far the place has outlived all the threats of demolition. There will remain a militant portion of citizens who will fight to retain the dear old City Hall.

The Isaac M. Wise Temple

T HE ISAAC M. WISE TEMPLE on Plum Street celebrated its centennial in 1966. It is still often referred to as the Plum Street Temple—it did not adopt the name of Rabbi Wise, who was responsible for its erection, until it was sixty-five years old.

Isaac Mayer Wise was a monumental figure in American Jewry and a leader in the cultural and intellectual history of Cincinnati. He came here in 1854 to lead the B'Nai Yeshurun congregation, which became the center of Reform Judaism in America. During his long career the rabbi was especially noted for starting the newspaper the *American Israelite* and founding the Hebrew Union College, the oldest Jewish theological school in the country. He was president of the college until his death.

Wise was not only instrumental in building the temple, he was responsible for its unique design. He called it an "Alhambra" temple. It is a mixture of architectural styles—Oriental, Moorish and Gothic, an example of "Jewish architecture," a short-lived style originated in Germany and adopted by Wise. It was the first temple of its kind in the nation. A few more of somewhat similar style were built in the East and then the fad was dropped.

So our temple is fascinatingly different and adds quite a touch of variety to the showplaces of the city.

The Cincinnati Woman's Club

In 1894 a half-dozen women met and formed the Cincinnati Woman's Club. Now it is a busy organization with many varied civic activities. Recently it has moved into a magnificent new home on Lafayette Avenue in Clifton but the club's beloved old place has not been forgotten.

Demolished in 1964 to make way for the Northeast Expressway, the beautiful clubhouse on Oak Street had become a landmark in Walnut Hills. The Georgian building of dark brick, with its dignified entrance, had been the meeting place for its thousand and more members since 1910. In 1935 the lovely walled garden, covering almost an acre of ground, had been added.

Upper Main Street

Every town has a Main Street, and Cincinnati's runs from the river north to the bordering hills—busy every step of the way. Until the turn of the century, the street ended in an incline which carried the streetcars majestically up the hill. Now flights of steps cover the site.

Looking down the street from Mulberry, the upper portion, which hasn't changed in many years, is seen as a crowded bit of the fringe area, stores and dwellings built snug and tight along the cluttered sidewalk.

In the distance the tall buildings of the downtown business district form a contrast for the older area.

The Eden Park Bridge

For over a century people have enjoyed the hills and drives of Eden Park. The first land for the project was purchased in 1859, and, since many acres of the rolling land were acquired from Nicholas Longworth, the park was named for his estate, "the Garden of Eden."

One of the familiar features of the place is the Melan Arch Bridge, which spans the traffic entering the park from Victory Parkway and the eastern hills. It was built in 1894 and was an achievement in engineering skill for its time, for it was the first bridge ever constructed of concrete.

Beyond the bridge, within the confines of the hundred and eighty-four acres, are some of the city's most popular cultural institutions. First, in sight of the entrance, there is the Krohn Conservatory with its elaborate displays, one of the finest greenhouses in the nation. Around the hill is the Art Museum and all its treasures, with the Art Academy and the Cincinnati Historical Society under its wing. It overlooks the reservoir and the Murray Seasongood Pavilion, where outdoor concerts have drawn crowds for many years. Newest of the attractions is the Playhouse in the Park, a professional theater, while the Museum of Natural History stands on the edge of the acreage at Gilbert Avenue.

The City from the Hills

The hills of Kentucky furnish the best vantage points from which to view the city. They also provide pleasant spots on which to give a moment's thought to the history of the little town on the river that grew and grew until it became a major city. There is even a high-rise now on the top of old Mount Adams.

It was the river, of course, winding through the valley, that influenced and determined the whole story. First it formed the borderline between the government-held lands of Kentucky and the Indian-held territory, a slowing-down hazard to the pioneers as they went pell-mell across the water in pursuit of marauding Indians.

Then the Ohio lands were opened for settlement and in that cold winter of 1788 the river became the road to the West for the crude flatboats that brought the apprehensive but hopeful first settlers. Next came Fort Washington and the Indian wars, then peace and more people, with the gradual spreading out, over and beyond the hills. The bridges were built and the buildings grew taller, closer together, filling up all the space.

It was all in a span of just one hundred and eighty years. Not a very long time between a wilderness and a city.

Mount Adams from Fort Washington Way

There used to be an incline to pull the streetcars up to Mount Adams. Pedestrians climbed steps to reach the top. Cars wound around circuitous routes. And it wasn't long ago that Eastern Avenue carried the full load of traffic to and from the eastern end of the city.

Now a network of cement strips crisscross the area under the hill—the approaches to the new distributor, Fort Washington Way.

Cincinnati has been working to improve her streets ever since Mr. McAdam invented a surface to cover the mud that mired down the carriage wheels and fill the holes that made the puddles that splashed a lady's trailing skirts. Considering that it was not until 1860 that the first ordinance was passed to keep the swine off the city's streets, Cincinnati has come a long way with her traffic problems.

Music Hall

Music hall on Elm Street, with all its turrets, towers and variety of ornamental design, is one of Cincinnati's most famous landmarks. The traditional center of the city's musical activity and best known today as the home of the symphony orchestra and the May Festival, the enormous place was opened in 1878 as one of the finest concert halls in the country, the acoustics of the auditorium world famous.

Originally the place was called Springer Auditorium, because, while it was built with contributions from many citizens, the greatest donor was Reuben R. Springer, who started the project.

Aside from the musical events, the great hall has welcomed, over the years, expositions, conventions, political rallies and a variety of activities which have drawn most of the city through its doors at one time or another. One of its early triumphs was in 1880 when the Democrats held their National Convention here, selecting General Winfield S. Hancock as their presidential candidate.

Large as it is, Music Hall has become inadequate for the growing needs of today's Cincinnati. A new convention center has been built closer to the downtown district. Only time will tell what effect this competition may have on the fine old building.

The Hamilton County Memorial Building

When a patriotic holiday comes around, attention is drawn to the Hamilton County Memorial Building. When a parade winds through the city it usually starts at the front door. Otherwise the elegant, ornate building seems to go unnoticed by most of the general public, even though it is used constantly for meetings of veterans' organizations and their auxiliaries. Possibly it is simply overshadowed by its huge, older neighbor, Music Hall. Both stand on Elm Street across from Washington Park and both were designed by the firm of architects, started by Samuel Hannaford, that designed so many of the public buildings in the city, including the City Hall, workhouse, and the old public library.

The Memorial Building was built in 1908 by the Grand Army of the Republic, then taken over by the county as a memorial to the military of the city and county. It contains mementoes, statues and pictures from the wars in which the nation has been involved.

A Monument in Fort Thomas

THE MILITARY POST which gave the city of Fort Thomas, Kentucky, its name no longer exists, but the tall tower which marked the entrance to the reservation is still very much in evidence. The massive shaft of rough-hewn limestone rising ninety feet into the air was built as a memorial to the local soldiers of the Spanish-American War by the citizens of Cincinnati, Covington, Newport and the area around the fort. Two antique cannons stand at the base, forged in Spain so long ago that they were more than a century old when captured in the Battle of San Juan Hill in 1898 and brought to Fort Thomas by American soldiers.

The post was established by Congress in 1887 after the nearby Newport Barracks was ruined by the great flood of 1884. The site of one hundred and twenty-five acres was chosen by General Philip Sheridan, who was sent from Washington to decide on a location. At the outbreak of the Spanish-American War the companies stationed here were sent to Cuba and the fort used as a mobilization center for troops readying for the war.

The fort has not been used as a military post for many years. It is now a Veterans Administration convalescent hospital and Army Reserve Center.

The Covington Cathedral Basilica

The superb Cathedral Basilica of the Assumption in Covington is a showplace for the whole area, unsurpassed in ecclesiastical beauty. Dedicated in 1910 after sixteen years in the building, it opened as Saint Mary's Cathedral. The towers were never finished to their full height but the façade was patterned after Notre Dame in Paris. The elaborate interior was inspired by the Abbey Church of Saint Denis. The great transept window is said to be one of the largest stained-glass windows in the world.

Foreign artisans were retained for the intricate details of the mosaics, wood carvings and stained glass but the mural on the walls of the Chapel of the Blessed Sacrament are by Covington's own Frank Duveneck. Cincinnati's famed sculptor, Clement Barnhorn, designed the elaborate bas-relief of the Assumption above the main door and the Madonna and Child in the central niche.

There is now a project to complete the twin towers and landscape the surroundings so that the magnificent building will rise above Madison Avenue in a park-like setting.

Fourth Street

Cincinnati's most familiar memorial to Abraham Lincoln is George Gray Barnard's great statue in Lytle Park. The well-known figure stands, year after year, facing the long length of Fourth Street.

Just how much the view has, or has not, changed with the years can be decided from the description of the street in Kenny's *Illustrated Cincinnati* published in 1875. It has this to say: "Fourth Street is pre-eminently the fashionable street of the city . . . on fine afternoons the sidewalks are thronged by as many as can be seen on any of the streets of New York . . . it is the constant resort of gayly dressed ladies out for a day's shopping, and is, in many respects, the main artery between the fashionable life of the East and West Ends."

The Clock on Fourth Street

There is a great flurry of changes going on all along Fourth Street from Race to Vine and Walnut. The one static fixture seems to be the old clock by the crosswalk between McAlpin's and Pogue's. It belongs to McAlpin's, which moved to the site in 1880, but many people who, year after year, have checked their watches with the time on its huge face, consider it a spontaneous appurtenance to the sidewalk. Fancy and all trimmed up with spidery metal scrollwork, the clock fits in nicely with all the programs to beautify the street.

This has always been a shopping center of great activity and growth. Now there is a giant new building for Closson's, a block-long garage for Pogue's, a remodeled façade for Gidding-Jenny, now combined, and Newstedt's has joined Loring Andrews. The fine old Sinton Hotel is gone but the impressive Provident Tower covers the corner.

These are all new today and will be taken for granted tomorrow. Their predecessors are almost forgotten. On this stretch of street some of the city's best have come and gone, moved away or disappeared. Once there was Pike's Opera House, the classic old Post Office, the St. Nicholas Hotel, Shillito's and the Neave Building. The famous Burnet House stood just around the corner.

The College-Conservatory

The Cincinnati Conservatory of Music, which was started by Miss Clara Baur and carried on by her niece, Miss Bertha Baur, began in a one-room studio in 1867. In 1902 it took over the John Shillito mansion, the ornate old building with marble floors, heavily carved woodwork and elaborate entrance built by Truman B. Handy during the Civil War. It became the nucleus of the many buildings which made up the campus of the school at Highland and Oak streets.

A few years ago the Conservatory and the College of Music, which dates back to 1878 and stood next to Music Hall for many years, combined to become the College-Conservatory. Now the school has reached another height in its ambitious history. It has become part of the University of Cincinnati and moved onto the Clifton campus. With appropriate ceremonies, in December of 1967, just one hundred years after its small beginning, its shining new complex was dedicated, the modern, fascinating, Corbett Center for the Performing Arts.

Sixth Street Market

Eagles over the doorway, a bell in the tower, circles and spires and fancy brickwork—that's the way they made a market house in the good old days. Markets were once of major importance, an essential part of the daily life of the city dwellers, the original cash-and-carry produce stores. Now with fresh fruit and vegetables easily available they have lost their prominent role.

The Jabez Elliot Flower Market, which ran from Elm to Plum, was closed in 1950 and then destroyed. Last year, as they widened Sixth Street, the old butchers' market house between Plum and Central was demolished. And so a little part of old-time Cincinnati disappeared, for this was the site of the Western Market, set aside for that purpose in the master plan for a growing city in 1892 and used continually through the many years.

Now, while around town a few of the open kiosks remain along the sidewalks, Findlay Market, on Elder Street, is the only enclosed market house left out of the many which once flourished.

Saint Rose Church

In this town, Saint Rose Church is not unique simply because it is a century old, carries an inscription in German over the door and is topped by a tall spire. It has become a favorite landmark because its location makes it so familiar to so many. From the winding curves of Columbia Parkway the spire is conspicuous for many miles as it rises against the city skyline. It is known to everyone who drives that busy artery. From the rear it is equally obvious to the men who travel up and down the river on boats. It is said that it is customary for them to check their watches with the tower clock every time they pass this point.

Saint Rose is on Eastern Avenue, in a section long known as Fulton, standing on a narrow plateau with the hills in front and the river at the back door. Fulton was a place of boatbuilding, very famous for the number and size of the steamboats turned out on its docks. The first great boom day was over in 1867 when the church was built, but the original members of the congregation were all connected with the industry in one way or another. So the old Ohio has always been part of the church's very existence and remains its constant companion—with tugs churning by on a summer day and the pleasure boats humming, through the bleak days of winter when icy winds blow off the water, and then spring, the season of floods with the cleanup time that follows. The first flood came before the building was really finished and sixty floods of various heights have threatened and sometimes entered the church in its one hundred years. A tall measuring stick on the rear of the building marks off the height and the time of the floods as they come and go.

An Old Mill

THE WATER-RUN MILL at the crossroads is a bit of vanishing Americana. Once they were found in every hamlet, usually the first enterprise established in each settlement, but they have long been superseded by grocery store packaged meal.

One of the rare mills which can be found today chugs merrily along in Friendship, Indiana, a small town near Madison. There has been a mill there since 1819; the present one built around seventy years ago over the first, which was lost by fire. There are three busy floors and a great turbine churning underneath. The water is diverted from Laughery Creek into a canal which passes under the mill to turn the wheels, and then goes on to empty into the creek farther downstream.

Crofton Drive

CROFTON DRIVE was just a small byway running off West St. Clair near Jefferson Avenue. It was a suburban alley that was unexpectedly picturesque as, warmed by sunlight, the high stone walls, twisting steps and abundant trees threw shadows across the narrow lane.

Recently there has been an amazing transformation around Clifton and Corryville. The great complex of the university is spreading out, the streets have been widened, new streets built, and the alley has suddenly disappeared in the maze of new buildings.

The Avalon

The steamer avalon, one of the last of the stern-wheelers, has left its Cincinnati dock down by the public landing. Once it was a packet on the Ohio and Mississippi rivers, then an excursion boat. Finally it was sold downriver to end its days as a museum piece at Louisville.

Instead it was renovated, named the *Belle of Louisville*, and graces the waterfront of that city. Each year, with great fanfare and exuberance, it races with Cincinnati's famous *Delta Queen*, the last of the steam-powered passenger boats on the inland waters. It's an uneven match but the smaller boat has become the pride of the Kentucky city and it is a festive day all around.

The two boats are among the last of their breed. Someday the far-sounding whistle of the "steamboat round the bend" will be a thing of the past—going the way of the girls in crinoline, the high beaver hats, the dueling pistols, and the chant of roustabouts—becoming just a bit of haunting American legend.

Stairs on Fort Washington Way

Cincinnati is noted for steps—and it keeps building more. Everyone is accustomed to the miles of cement stairways climbing the rugged cliffs around the edge of the city. Down in the basin area, where the terrain is comparatively flat, they are not expected. Now, with all the construction going on, the bulldozers have built up slopes where there was only a gradual rise before. And so there are steps. Typical of the new landscape is the view from the end of the Suspension Bridge where a nice, new cement flight goes up a smooth but steep man-made slope to Fort Washington Way at the end of Vine Street.

The Monument to Fort Washington

The city's only monument to Fort Washington can be found, if one knows where to look, on the grassy bank of the new expressway distributor, Fort Washington Way. The marker says that the post was three hundred feet northeast of the spot.

The rather insignificant memento to the city's beginning, now remade and the inscription revised, is simply a granite-log representation of one of the bastions of the old fort. Put up in 1900 by the patriotic societies of Ohio, it stood in the center of Third Street at Ludlow until it was removed to make way for the distributor. Now it has been determined by the Historical Society that even before it was moved it was not on the correct site, that the fort extended from Fourth to Third Street but did not extend across the street as was originally supposed.

The story of Fort Washington and the settlement which became Cincinnati is well known. There were three rival spots on the banks of the Ohio, between the Great and Little Miami Rivers, that enticed the pioneers—Columbia, Cincinnati and North Bend. The fascinating John Cleves Symmes was proprietor of all and he picked North Bend as the most promising and as his choice for the government's fort. However, it was at the site opposite the Licking River, the more central location, that Major Doughty, in 1789, established his little company of soldiers for the protection of the territory. History tells of the rivalry between the soldiers and the civilians, the conflict over the relative importance of military and civil officers of the small community but there is no doubt that it was only because of military protection that the town prospered and grew. It was because old Fort Washington was built here that Cincinnati stands where she is today.

Tomb of William Henry Harrison

The tomb of William Henry Harrison, on a hillside in North Bend, Ohio, can be seen for miles around, from the highway and from the river. It is Ohio's memorial to the ninth President of the United States.

There are not too many memorials, around the city, to the man who died one month after taking office as President. There is a town, a school and an avenue bearing his name, and the statue across from the public library. He was considered a native son of Ohio, though he was born in Virginia, at beautiful "Berkely," home of his father Benjamin, one-time governor of Virginia and signer of the Declaration of Independence. He came to Cincinnati at the age of seventeen as an ensign at Fort Washington and from then on his life was centered around the area. While he was kept away by some of the many offices he held, as general in the Army, governor of the Northwest Territory, Congressman and Senator, he had married the daughter of John Cleves Symmes at North Bend and that was where he had his home. There, too, in this small community, some twenty miles out of Cincinnati, his grandson Benjamin, who became the twenty-third President, was born.

When Harrison died in 1841, the solemn funeral was held at Christ Church on Fourth Street. Then the steamboat *Raritan*, followed by three others filled with townspeople, carried the body downstream to North Bend. An unpretentious tomb was erected.

In the 1920s the Ohio Legislature appropriated funds for a more stately memorial. Now, the simple but impressive shaft stands in a small state park. Wide flagstone steps, guarded by massive eagles and a lone pine tree, lead to the rather isolated spot high above the bend in the Ohio River, far from the rumbling of war, the strife of political life.

From Log Cabin to High-rise

~~~~~~~~◆~~~~~~~~

Where but in Cincinnati would you find a high-rise apartment and a log cabin on the same hilltop? This happy contrast of the old and new can be seen in East Walnut Hills where the River Terrace Apartments stand on the crest of the hill at the end of Ingleside Avenue while the log cabin sits on the side of the overhanging slope that descends down toward Columbia Parkway. They both have expansive views of the river.

The cabin was on the hillside when the John R. Bullocks sold their home and land for the modern complex. It is an authentic old log house, almost a century old, and it once stood out in the country. When W. J. Williams, president of the Western-Southern Life Insurance Company, owned the two-and-a-half-acre estate, he had it dismantled, brought to the suburb and re-erected log by log as a playhouse for his granddaughter. Now it serves as a charming residence.

Ortiz Alley

As vine street twists and turns its climbing way from Clifton Avenue to McMicken, short streets veer off into the craggy bluffs which border its path. One is a shadowy little place which boasts no street sign to give its name but is listed in the directory as Ortiz Alley. It's just a quaint byway that cuts in between the houses above Hollister, a pocket in the hillside, making room for more houses on a slope that some might feel too steep for habitation.

The Cincinnati Academy of Medicine

The Cincinnati Academy of Medicine now has its own permanent home on Broadway below Fourth. Founded in 1857, the organization has moved many times, never before owning its own meeting place.

The new headquarters is the big house with the twin entrances next to the University Club, one of the town houses of an earlier decade built when materials were plentiful and cheap, and craftsmen were painstaking with every detail. It dates back to 1850. It was the home of Christopher G. Pearce, captain of an Ohio River steamboat and later president of the United States Mail Line, which carried the mail up and down the river to and from Louisville.

Elsinore Entrance

It may seem strange to use the word "whimsical" in connection with anything as massive as the stone gateway known as the Elsinore Entrance to Eden Park, but if the city ever made a spontaneous, impulsive gesture it was when the Water Works Department patterned its new valve house after a stage setting in a production of Hamlet.

The story goes that just when it needed a valve house for the affluent mains, which could also serve as an entrance to the park from Gilbert Avenue, James E. Murdoch was appearing in the Shakespearean drama. That seemed to be enough. There were no years of study, no competitive plans. It was simply built like the make-believe castle in the backdrop.

Today the entrance is sometimes called a monstrosity, a horrible example of the architectural style of its day, but it is quaint, it's impressively large and it's cherished by many as one of Cincinnati's own original creations.

The University of Cincinnati

The University of Cincinnati becomes steadily larger with each year. There is more and more construction to meet the growing needs. It is one of the largest municipal universities in the country and the second oldest. Fourteen colleges now make up the complex. From Burnet Woods can be seen an example of the variety of its buildings, the glass walls of the Applied Arts College and the tower of familiar McMicken Hall in the distance.

McMicken Hall is the second building of that name on this site. The first, built in 1898, was also the first building on the campus. It honored Charles McMicken, who, in 1858, left his estate to be used for an institution of higher education, a gift that helped make the great university a reality.

Hamer and Back Streets

Just a stone's throw from the bustle of upper Vine, Hamer and Back Streets meet in as quaint a little corner as can be found downtown. This is part of the small triangular section of neat brick buildings and narrow streets between Vine Street and McMicken which was known once as the Northern Liberties. Near here was the old canal, and Mohawk, and earlier still, the place where Mrs. Trollope lived when she moved out of the city to the country for her "rusticity."

Early maps show McMicken as Hamilton Road, Hamer as Pleasant, but Back Street was known by that name at least as long ago as the map of 1819.

Benton Street

Benton street cuts across the tip of the small triangular section squeezed in between Vine and McMicken. It's a bit of Cincinnati that looks just as it did in the latter days of the last century. Few new buildings break the endless compact rows of sturdy brick houses, stores and occasional breweries.

Benton is typical of the streets that border McMicken, a thoroughfare with a character all its own. It travels from east to west and then north in a winding course around the base of the hill topped by Fairview Heights and Clifton. It extends from Main Street to Hopple. Once it went on through Cumminsville as part of the old Hamilton Road, which was beaten into a highway by soldiers marching up the Millcreek Valley from Fort Washington to Hamilton and on into northwestern Ohio. They were following an old Indian trail. This part of the avenue was renamed for Charles McMicken, one of the founders of the University of Cincinnati.

From the Covenant-First Presbyterian Church

THE COVENANT-FIRST PRESBYTERIAN CHURCH stands at the corner of Eighth and Elm fronting a vista of Garfield Place and Piatt Park from its grilled gates on Elm Street. The park is the oldest in the city, the acre of ground having been given by John and Benjamin Piatt in 1817. It was originally intended for a marketplace, but as early as 1843 it was enclosed with a high iron fence and used as a park. It was named for Garfield when the statue of the President was erected, but finally, in 1940, it was renamed Piatt Park.

Seen from the east, the church is one of the historic buildings which make up the lovely skyline at the end of Eighth Street. The spires of Saint Peter's, a bit of the Plum Street Temple and City Hall rise beyond the square stone towers of the church.

Elgin Place

ELGIN PLACE is one of the short hill streets of Mount Adams. Here it is seen through the trees of Eden Park as it meets Paradome Street and Parkside Place, with the Holy Cross Monastery covering the top of the hill beyond.

A closer view of Holy Cross Church and the monastery tower can be obtained from Saint Paul Place.

The monastery stands on the site of the old observatory, and the observatory was the building which started the hilltop community on its way when Nicholas Longworth gave four acres of land for its construction. Mount Adams was named when former President John Quincy Adams came to town in 1843 to dedicate the building.

Along the River

Little harbors are scattered all along the banks of the Ohio with pleasure boats ready for summer weekend relaxation. Every year the river attracts more enthusiasts to take advantage of the water at the city's front door.

Extensive plans are now being completed to beautify the riverfront. Markland Dam has raised the pool stage, and more and more activity is anticipated. Restaurants and marinas dot the shoreline from New Richmond to Saylor Park and the buzzing hum of motorboats of every size and description fills the air.

The river has come a long way since it was the "highway of the pioneers" and every boat was purely utilitarian, beginning with the flatboats, keelboats and poled rafts coming down the current from the old home back East, with the cow and some chickens, as well as grandma's rocking chair and the cradle for the baby.

Aurora from Hillforest

Aurora, Indiana, is one of the most charming of the river towns close to Cincinnati. It is a place of shady streets running along and up the hillsides, century-old churches, pleasant houses overlooking a great curve in the Ohio, and a ferryboat that goes back and forth to Petersburg, Kentucky. It is also the birthplace of Edwin C. Hill and Elmer Davis, writers and radio commentators.

Aurora is one of the early Dearborn County settlements. Twenty-some miles from Cincinnati, not far from North Bend and opposite the open lands of Kentucky, there were pioneers along Hogan and Laughery creeks before the land was offered for sale in 1800. It was a rugged trip through the forest from the other settlements but an inviting spot for those who approached from the river. So it grew rapidly. It became a town, formally, in 1819 and was named for the goddess of the dawn.

The most flourishing period in the town's history was during the steamboat and stagecoach era. The most imposing of the houses were built during that time. One mansion is "Hillforest," now a museum owned by the Hillforest Historical Foundation. Built in the style of an Italian villa by Thomas Gaff in the 1850s, it is always described as "steamboat Gothic," its rounded cupola comparable to the pilot-houses of the steamers. From here Mr. Gaff could watch the steamboats, his own among them, as they traveled the river, but the view was also excellent from the windows of the house and from between the slender pillars of the front portico.

The Fort Hamilton Monument

Approaching hamilton, ohio, from the west, one sees the Soldiers' Memorial Building, across the Miami River, dominating the view of the downtown area. The building, topped by a statue of a Civil War soldier, contains relics and records of all the nation's wars and is a memorial to the local soldiers, sailors and pioneers who participated. At the base stand the stone-log replicas of the corner bastions of old Fort Hamilton.

It was in 1791 that General St. Clair, in his disastrous march north from the Ohio River to subdue the Indians, established the fort at the crossing of the Great Miami. He named it for Alexander Hamilton. It was to be used as a base for supplies and as the first stopover point from his headquarters at Fort Washington. Two years later General Anthony Wayne, following the same trail in his successful campaign which ended in the battle of Fallen Timbers, used and built up the fort. It contained a barracks for two hundred soldiers, with a stockade fifty yards square.

A town soon developed around the post, the squares laid off by Israel Ludlow, and it was named Hamilton. When a county grew up around the town it became the seat of government. Soon the town became a city. Today it is an important Miami Valley industrial and business center but a city conscious of its heritage, taking pride in protecting a sampling of its progressive years.

The Steeple of Philippus Church

From the Clifton Avenue Hill the giant hand which tops Philippus Evangelical and Reformed Church is seen high above Race Street and the city. The giant golden fist with index finger pointing to heaven is one of the last of the quaint symbols of the old-time, Over the Rhine, German section of Cincinnati which have been viewed affectionately by many, many people through the years.

The church stands facing the length of Race Street at Ohio and McMicken, built in 1890 as "Philippus Kirche." It was one of the last churches in which German was spoken exclusively. The congregation adopted the English language for its sermons in 1921.